Cacti & Su[...]
for Moder[...]

MW01006047

Contents

Introduction. 2
What are cacti and succulents?. 2
Botanical naming of cacti and succulents. 2-3
Buying cacti and succulents. 3
Adjusting succulents to indoor conditions. 4
Growth cycles in cacti and succulents. 4-5
LIGHT. 5
    Bright. 5
    Moderate. 5
    Dim. 5
    Artificial light. 5
WATER. 6
    Watering methods. 6
Temperature. 7
Fertilizer. 7
Soils. 8
Containers and repotting. 8
Cacti and succulents outdoors. 9
PROPAGATION. 9
    Cuttings and offsets. 9-10
    Cacti from seed. 10
Flowering of cacti. 11
Cactus and succulent problems. 12-13
Acknowledgements. 14
Cacti illustrations and care instructions. 15-41
Succulent illustrations and care instructions. 42-77
Index. 78-80

Publisher's representative for distribution in Canada. Horta Craft Ltd., London, Ontario.

1

0-89484-003-7

Introduction

Cacti and succulents are among the most unique and fascinating types of indoor plants. Through millions of years of evolution, they have developed amazing methods of water storage and self protection which enable them to survive in some of the most inhospitable growing areas on earth.

For indoor plants, cacti and succulents are the perfect choice. Typical hot, dry indoor conditions are often harmful to leafy foliage plants, but provide the ideal climate for many kinds of succulent plants. In addition, these remarkable plants are very tolerant of neglect, requiring little watering or other care throughout the greater part of the year. The results of such benign neglect are often large, colorful blossoms, an added bonus whenever they appear.

Outdoors, cacti and succulents are a handsome addition in the landscape or in containers on a patio in summer. Although most are not frost hardy, a few will survive even the coldest of winter climates.

No matter what your taste, cacti and succulents have the diversity and adaptability to suit almost any lifestyle. A small investment will reward you with enjoyment for many years.

What are Cacti and Succulents?

A succulent is generally considered to be any plant which has the natural ability to store water in its body or roots. Succulents usually have fattened leaves or thick stems filled with stored water, which allow them to live through long periods without moisture. Their swollen bodies and general lack of normal, thin leaves cause them to have much less surface exposed to the air from which moisture can evaporate. Their unique adaptation also enables succulent plants to store water, when it is available, quickly and in great volume, using it internally as needed.

Although many succulents are adapted to dry locations where rainfall is scarce, some (such as Christmas Cactus) are native to moist, tropical forests, and live high in trees, rooted to the bark. Still others are found at high elevations in the mountains where temperatures drop extremely low, and others along ocean shores where they are exposed to heavy fogs and occasional sea spray.

True cacti are one type of succulent; they are members of the plant family Cactaceae. All cacti are native to the Western Hemisphere, and although many bear spines, this characteristic alone does not make them cacti. Many succulents other than cacti also bear spines, such as Crown of Thorns. A true cactus is distinguished by the presence of areoles, small nubbin-like structures which occur over the body of the plant. Cactus spines, as well as roots and flowers, always grow from these areoles, whereas spines on succulents other than cacti grow directly out of the body of the plant.

Botanical Naming of Cacti and Succulents

Botanical naming of plants is necessary for several reasons. First, botanical names are an international language, standard throughout the world. Common names are very inconsistent, and two completely different plants can both be correctly referred to by the same common name. For example, Ferocactus acanthodes and Echinocactus grusonii are both called Barrel Cactus, although they are not the same plant. Accordingly, if you need to order a specific plant by mail, using the correct botanical name is the only way to make certain you will receive the plant you want. Secondly, not all plants have common names, particularly if they are not commonly grown. In these cases the botanical name of a plant is the only one available.

Botanical naming is not that difficult. Plant names always consist of at least two words; the first is the genus and the second the specific epithet. Together, the two words are referred to as the species. Related plants may all belong to the same genus (for example, Sedum rubrotinctum—Christmas Cheers and Sedum morganianum—Burro Tail p. 73), but they will never have the same specific epithet.

To put it another way, a genus can be compared to a person's last name (Smith) and the specific epithet to his first name (John or Fred). John and Fred Smith would be related, but would obviously not be the same person. In the same way, 2 plants in the same genus would be similar in some ways but not identical.

Any words appearing beyond the two part standard botanical name identify a plant as being slightly different from the basic species. It might have brighter flowers or a faster growth rate, for example. These variety or cultivar names, as they are called, are separated from the remainder of the botanical name by the letter "v" or single quotes.

Looking toward broader classifications, there are plant families. These families group more than one genus together and signify that all plants in those genera (plural of genus) are similar in some basic way. All plants found in the first half of this book belong to one family, the cactus family, but the succulent plant section takes in many different families.

As a final note, an "x" or the word hybrid appearing with a botanical name indicates that the plant is a cross between two other plants.

Buying Cacti and Succulents

Succulent plants tend to be somewhat more expensive than most common foliage plants, and if you are investing a moderate amount of money, some guidelines on selecting quality plants will be helpful.

There are many places where plants can be purchased: groceries, discount stores, plant shops, florists, garden centers, or professional succulent nurseries. Any of these places may be a source of quality plants, but you may have to pick and choose carefully to find them. Groceries and discount stores will usually carry small plants at inexpensive prices, but often do not have proper conditions to grow them until they are sold. Accordingly, it is advisable to buy from them only plants which have been recently received. Plant shops, florists, and garden centers have larger and more expensive plants, and are a more reliable source of quality plants. For best quality and selection, a professional succulent grower is the best choice. Plants will generally be correctly identified and well grown, and you will be able to obtain growing information for the plant. Ordering from a succulent grower's catalog is a good way to obtain quality plants, as there is usually a large assortment of kinds to choose from, and cacti and succulents ship well over long distances.

A few points to remember when selecting cacti and succulents are:

1. Beware of buying large, full-grown cacti at bargain prices. They are often dug from the desert and their roots severed. Such plants are very difficult for most people to reroot and will usually die a slow death over many months.

2. Check the base of plants at the soil line for signs of softness and discoloration. These are sure signs of rot, a disease which destroys the roots of cacti and succulents. Plants infected with rot may be cured by cutting off and rerooting the remaining healthy portion of the body (see problems section p. 78)

but it is always wiser not to purchase an obviously diseased plant.

3. Avoid plants with new growth which is thin and pale in color. These signs tell that the plants have been poorly grown and are in a weakened condition. Such plants will never completely regain a normal, healthy appearance.

4. Check thoroughly for insects, particularly scale and mealy bugs (see page 78 for descriptions). One insect-infested plant can infect an entire collection of succulents very quickly.

Other than these occasionally occuring problems, cacti and succulents are nearly free of insect and disease problems.

Adjusting Succulents to Indoor Conditions

Plants which are bought already potted should be placed initially in light at about the same intensity at which they were growing when purchased. They can then be gradually moved to higher light as required for the particular species without danger of sunburn (see page 5). Watering will be determined by the time of year at which the plant is received. Plants bought in their dormant season should be watered only very lightly every few weeks, while plants which are actively growing should be kept slightly moist and and not allowed to stay dry for more than 2-3 days.

Plants which are received unpotted should first have the roots carefully inspected for insects and diseases, and all damaged and broken roots should be carefully trimmed off with scissors. The plants should then be potted in the correct soil mix (see soils page 8), watered lightly to aid the roots in becoming re-established, and placed out of direct sun for several weeks before being moved slowly to stronger light.

Growth Cycles in Cacti and Succulents

In their natural state, most plants undergo growing and resting cycles on a yearly basis. Most cacti and succulents respond to both temperature and rainfall, having at one time of year a dormant season when temperatures are cool and rain scarce, and later a growing season with warm temperatures and abundant rain. Knowing each plant's growth and rest cycles is important in determining its care requirements for best health and growth.

Most cacti and many succulents have their active growth period during spring and summer, gradually slowing growth to become dormant in fall and winter. Plants with this type of growth cycle include: Echinocactus and Ferocactus (the Barrel Cacti), Astrophytum, Opuntia, and many others. These plants should be kept warm and well watered during their natural growing season, and cool and quite dry at other times of the year.

The tree dwellers, called epiphytes, are another type of cactus requiring particular cyclic care. Although they are fleshy, succulent appearing plants, they are not adapted to full sun as other cacti, being native to shady jungles. They are also not as tolerant of drought as the round-bodied, desert dwelling cacti. The schlumbergera, rhipsalidopsis, and epiphyllum genera are members of this group. Some, such as Christmas Cactus (Schlumbergera) are winter blooming, while others like Easter Cactus (Rhipsalidopsis) are spring blooming. They are best kept moist and warm throughout the late spring and summer growing season, but cool and dry for the several months preceeding yearly flowering.

Certain succulents from South Africa (collectively called Mesembs for short) have a peculiar growing pattern all their own. They have a long dormant period through most of the summer, while growing in winter. (This is more easily understood if you recall that seasons in their native South Africa are reversed from the Northern hemisphere) Water must be given extremely sparingly during this summer dormant period or rotting will be unavoidable. Light spraying and never completely wetting the soil are the best watering methods.

No matter what type of plant you have or which growth cycle it follows, four aspects of care must be balanced to grow any plant successfully: light, water, temperature, and fertilizer.

Light

The amount of light given to cacti and succulents is one of the most important factors in their growth. For this reason, each plant species or genus in this book has its light requirements listed in the care information section. The terms used in those sections are explained more fully below so that you can locate your plant in an area which receives the proper amount of light.

Bear in mind that the light requirements listed below are only recommendations, and that some cacti and succulents will grow in less light if adjusted gradually and watered and fertilized sparingly to correspond to the lower light.

Bright Light

The majority of cacti and succulents require strong sunlight to grow well. As a rule, plants listed as requiring bright light should be grown directly in a window. Windows facing South provide the most light, and cactus and succulent collections have flourished in such a location for many years. East or West windows offer the next light intensity, with direct sun for at least part of the day. Northern windows are dimmest, receiving no direct sun, only indirect, reflected light. In the summer bright light plants should be grown outdoors in full sun.

Moderate Light

A number of cacti and succulents will grow in moderate light with some direct sun. These plants generally grow well up to 3 feet (1M) from south, east, or west windows.

Dim Light

Few of the plants in this book are recommended for dim light (more than 4 feet from windows), however many may survive at low light intensities for months, slowly becoming weaker with spindly pale growth.

Your own judgement is the best indicator of whether your plant is receiving too little or too much light. In "sun belt" areas of the country south or west windows may give too much light. In other situations roof overhangs, trees, constant cloud cover, or smog may block out most of the direct light. Watch for the symptoms of excess and insufficient light listed on page 78 to guide you in giving each plant its proper amount of light.

Artificial Light

Many people interested in succulent plants lack sufficient natural light to successfully grow them. In other cases a cactus and succulent fancier may have a rapidly expanding collection which has outgrown the available window space. In these instances, artificial light is the obvious answer. There are many brands of plant lights available, and many cacti and succulent plants will flourish under them. Another method is suspending a 2 tube cool white fluorescent fixture over your plant collection. The light given off is satisfactory for growing, but you may not be able to readily flower your succulent plants in it.

Water

Although cacti and succulents are adapted to withstand dry conditions, this does not mean they are unaffected by or immune to underwatering. During their growth periods (usually spring and summer) they absorb moisture rapidly and may need to be watered every 1-3 days. Growth will be best if the soil is only allowed to partially dry between waterings. All the soil should be wet thoroughly at each watering and then allowed to dry to a point where it contains only a small amount of moisture before being rewet. It is nearly impossible to prescribe how many days should pass between waterings because the rate of soil drying varies so much between plants. For example, room temperature, soil makeup, root system size, and pot material will all speed up or slow down the drying process. Your best clue of when to water is the feel of the soil. When you suspect a plant needs water, push your fingers into the soil about ½ inch (1 cm) deep. A cool or damp feeling means that there is still moisture in the soil. By testing the soil this way several times, you will be able to judge how many days should pass between waterings.

Water given during the plant's dormant season (usually fall and winter) should be applied more sparingly. Your cacti, and many succulents, are not actively growing and will be very susceptible to overwatering damage. A light watering every few weeks after the soil has thoroughly dried is best, applying just enough water to dampen the roots slightly and keep the plants from shriveling. Do not soak all the soil in the pot.

Watering Methods

Most people water their plants from above, directly onto the soil. For many this is a perfectly satisfactory method. It is wise, however, not to wet the body of a cactus, since the water may remain in the top of some barrel or other oddly shaped plant encouraging rot problems to develop. By the same token, it is best to water in the morning, so that any water spilled on the cactus will evaporate rapidly in the sunlight.

Another watering method useful in some situations is bottom watering. However, since it completely wets the soil, it should not be used to water dormant plants. Bottom watering is a useful way to water large round bodied cacti that nearly fill the top of a pot. Top watering such plants often only lets water flow down the sides of the pot, leaving the soil beneath the plant and surrounding the roots bone dry.

Secondly, cacti and succulents are sometimes bought already potted in a soil mix largely composed of peat moss. When the peat is allowed to dry completely, it will not absorb water poured on from above. The water will run through quickly, leaving the bulk of the soil unwetted. The peat can be most successfully rewet by the gradual wicking action found with bottom watering. To bottom water a cactus or succulent, submerge the pot in water up to its rim for 10-20 minutes. Water will enter through the drainage holes slowly and saturate the soil. Then, allow the soil to drain before replacing the plant in its growing location.

Another method of bottom watering is by filling the plant saucer with water repeatedly until no more is absorbed. Be sure to dump any excess water left in the saucer promptly! Your plants should never be allowed to stand in water.

One hazard of bottom watering is the build up of excess fertilizer which is not washed out of the soil as it is when a plant is watered from above. Accordingly, it is wise to fertilize bottom-watered plants less often; and at a weaker strength. Watering from above every 5-8 waterings will help rinse extra fertilizer out, and is a precaution which should be taken if your plants are routinely bottom watered.

6

Temperature

Cacti and succulent plants tolerate a wide range of temperatures, from near freezing in the winter to 95°F (35°C) in summertime. The proper temperature is dependent on whether the plant is growing or dormant. Dormant plants should be grown at temperatures from 45-55°F (7-10°C). An enclosed porch or unheated bedroom is often a good place for wintering succulents or cacti. The cool temperatures combined with only light, occasional waterings "harden" the plants, making them stronger and healthier. In addition, flower buds are likely to form at cool temperatures. Many people do not have a room which is much cooler than normal, or simply don't want to shut their decorative succulent plants in an out of the way place. In this case, keeping the plants on a windowsill is a partial substitute. Cold temperatures can make the area right by the window 5-10°F (2-3°C) cooler than the rest of the room. Be careful, however, of shutting drapes over the plants at night. The cold air can become trapped and create frost.

Growing at normal indoor temperatures during the winter dormant period will by no means kill a plant. Many will in fact thrive for years without any cool period. Cool temperatures are suggested only because they are best for most cacti and for some succulent plants, approaching normal outdoor growing conditions. Convenience and personal preference will decide the winter temperature at which your succulent plants are grown.

The summer preferences of cacti and succulents are an easy matter. Room temperatures up to 95°F (35°C) are fine, just so long as moisture is supplied, sometimes daily on very hot days. Plants summered outdoors will do fine in shifting day and night temperatures as long as there is no frost.

Fertilizer

Cacti and succulents do not live on light and water alone. They need fertilizer the same as other plants, but in smaller amounts. Fertilizing should be done only while plants are actively growing, which is generally during spring and summer.

Liquid or water soluble fertilizers are a good choice for succulent plants. They can be used several times each growing season in normal watering and their nutrients will be quickly available to the plants.

Time release or pelleted fertilizers are also good. Most release fertilizer for 3-4 months, so you can apply them at the start of the growing season and fertilizing chores for the year are complete. The pellets will slowly release fertilizer at each watering, and be used up by the time your plant enters its dormant period.

Of the three components of a fertilizer: nitrogen, phosphorous and potassium, the middle one, phosphorus, is most important. The front of a fertilizer container usually lists three numbers separated by dashes: e.g. 10-10-10 or 10-15-15. These indicate the percentages of the 3 components — nitrogen, phosphorus and potassium in the fertilizer. When choosing a cactus fertilizer, try to find a low nitrogen content (first number) and a high phosphorous content (middle number). Formulas such as 5-10-5, 10-20-10, 10-20-20, or 5-10-10 are fine.

Blooming houseplant or African Violet fertilizers usually contain a correct formula. Fertilizer is not a cure-all for unhealthy plants, in fact, a dose of fertilizer on a plant already in poor condition could kill it. Also, never fertilize a newly transplanted or acquired plant. Such plants need at least one month to adjust before being fertilized.

Soils

Soil mixes for cacti and succulents are of two types: sandy mixes for most arid-area cacti and succulents and humusy combinations for tree dwelling or jungle cacti. In either soil mix, good drainage is most important.

Prepared soil mixes sold specifically for use with arid cacti are readily available. Some are good, others not so good. Try to avoid those containing lots of peat moss. When they dry thoroughly, (as they should in winter) they are practically waterproof, and must be slowly rewet by soaking.

Jungle cacti do not need the sandy soil used by most cacti and succulents. They will do well in any general house plant soil mix, designed for foliage plants since they are naturally used to the large amounts of peat and humus found in almost all prepared mixes.

Making your own soil mixes is a good idea. For arid species, a combination of one part coarse builders sand (not sea sand!), one part garden soil (without clay), and one part peat moss makes a fine mix. As another alternative, equal parts prepared house plant soil and sand is just as good. For jungle cacti, one part sand, one part garden soil, and two parts peat is a good balance.

Containers and Repotting

For cactus and succulent growing, plain unglazed clay pots are the traditional choice. They are inexpensive, have drainage holes, and allow soil to dry evenly by the evaporation of water through the sides. In short, they provide the best conditions for growth at an inexpensive price.

On the other hand, decorative pots can enhance the character of a plant and make it an attractive decorating item. Cacti and succulents can be grown just as successfully in these decorative pots; you will just have to be more careful in watering.

Repotting of cacti and succulents should be done as needed by the plant rather than on any particular yearly schedule. Most succulent type plants are slow growing enough that they only need larger pots every 3 to 5 years or so. Many people repot their plants too often, needlessly disturbing the roots, when increasing the fertilizing frequency would have worked just as well.

You can often determine if a plant needs repotting by simply looking at the size of the plant in comparison to its present pot. If the plant is top heavy and easily tips over, it is probably time to repot, but as a double check you may want to look at the roots. To do this first gently turn the pot upside down; hold the plant and soil in with your other hand. Tap the edge of the pot on a counter or other surface, and the soil and roots should slide out undisturbed. If you see a great number of roots entirely filling the pot it is time to move to a larger container.

Always repot into a container only slightly larger than the present one, placing a broken piece of pot over the drainage hole to keep the soil in. For pots without drainage holes, a layer of gravel in the pot will provide a catchbasin for excess water and keep it away from the roots.

In transplanting, try to set the plant at the same level it was originally growing, and fill in around it with damp soil. Do not water immediately; wait several days to a week before watering to allow time for any damaged roots to heal. Water sparingly for the next few weeks.

Cacti and Succulents Outdoors

For summertime container planting on a porch or patio, cacti and succulent plants are ideal. Most kinds will thrive in the fresh air, sunshine, and warm temperatures of summer, requiring little care and providing enjoyment all season.

When moving cacti and succulents from indoor growing conditions to a more brightly lit outdoor situation, a period of adjustment is essential. Otherwise, your plants will become severely sun damaged and lose their healthy appearance. Move them first to a lightly shaded outdoor area which receives only a little direct sun daily. After a week or two, move to a brighter area, and after that to full sun.

Remember that not all cacti and succulents are sun lovers. Jungle cacti such as Schlumbergera and Rhipsalis are better in shade and will grow best hung under trees where they will receive only filtered sunlight.

Propagation

Cuttings and Offsets

The main ways in which cacti and succulents are propagated are by cuttings, seeds, and offsets. To decide which way is the proper one to propagate your plant, first look at the way it grows.

A branching growth style is characteristic of many succulent plants. Jade plants and kalanchoes are two examples. Many members of the cactus family also branch, such as opuntias and Rhipsalidopsis. For plants of this type, propagation is easy; just cut off several segments (on Rhipsalidopsis) or the tip of a stem and you have a cutting which can be easily rooted to give a new plant.

Other succulents grow in a "rosette" form, with all the leaves growing from a central point and overlapping each other in a rose petal-like fashion. Echeverias, sedums, and pachyphytums show up in this group. In plants of this type, a single detached, healthy leaf will often root and develop a new plant at the base. More often, however, rosette plants produce young plants on their own in the form of "offsets" or "pups". Offsets are found growing at the base of the parent plant, being attached to it by either an aboveground or underground stem. Agaves and sansevierias are two succulents which commonly have offsets.

Offsets or pups found at the base of a plant may be removed in several ways. The most common is division, in which the entire plant with attached pups is taken out of its pot and gently broken apart into individual plants, each containing its own root system. As an alternative when only one offset is growing, it may be easier to dig out the small plant without unpotting the parent. If an underground stem is connecting the pup to the parent it must be cut, and this is easiest accomplished by pushing a knife deep into the soil near the offset on the side next to the parent plant. Digging or lifting the pup out after that will be relatively easy. Many offsets have well developed root systems of their own, especially if they have been visible and growing for several months. These may be potted immediately. Those which don't have roots should be treated like unrooted cuttings.

Still other succulents and cacti grow in clusters, producing small plants (offsets) in great numbers around the original plant. Some mammillarias, gymnocalyciums and fenestrarias grow in this way, with some (such as echinopsis) actually developing young plants all over the body of the parent. In these cases, smaller plants generally break off readily and can be rooted easily. Often, they will have already grown roots while still attached.

The technique for rooting and growing new plants from leaves, cuttings, pups, offsets and the like is not complicated. First, any thick-stemmed cuttings with large cut surfaces should be left to air dry out of direct sun for up to two weeks. This drying period allows the cut area to "heal". This healing (called callousing) helps discourage rotting when the base is buried in the rooting material. Leaves and small cuttings do not need to be dried, and can be stuck immediately into the rooting mixture.

Many materials may be used for rooting cacti and succulents, sand, pumice, cactus soil mix, or vermiculite for example. A mixture of sand and vermiculite is one excellent choice since it is sterile, drains quickly, and yet holds some moisture to start the rooting process. To root your cutting or offset, just cover the base with damp rooting mix, set in a bright area (but not in full, direct sun) and wait, keeping the rooting mix always slightly damp. Roots will form in a few weeks if all is well. Leaves from which you wish to form new plants should be treated in the same way, except that they should be laid on top of the rooting mix instead of being pushed down into it. When the roots of a cutting, offset or leaf are well developed, you will feel a slight resistance when the piece is pulled. It will then be ready for potting up as a normal plant.

Cacti and Succulents from Seed

Growing plants from seed is an interesting experiment, if nothing else, and it is also the only way to propagate cacti which do not form offsets easily. If one of your own plants has set seed, growing it first is one way to start. Later you may want to order seed from a professional cactus seed specialist.

To harvest cactus seeds, just open the seed pod (fruit) and separate the seed from the pulp, allowing it to dry on a paper towel. Since many succulent plant seeds germinate normally during wet spring weather, this is a good time to start seed indoors. Your plants will be able to take advantage of the strong summer sun to become well established by fall.

Although cuttings may be rooted in pure sand, seeds should be sown in a richer mix since the seedlings will be growing in the same soil mix for 6 months to a year. One good seed mix may be made by combining equal parts of sand, soil, and finely shredded peat moss. As a precaution against soil borne diseases, the soil should be sterilized before use. Dampen it slightly and bake loosely covered with foil at 350°F (176°C) for 35 minutes.

Fill a plastic pot with cooled, moistened mix and sprinkle the seed over the surface. Barely cover with more soil mix sifted through a strainer for fineness. Next, submerge the pot in water up to its rim to allow water to flow up through the drainage holes and dampen the soil; drain and cover with plastic wrap to seal in the moisture. A warm, well-lit area without direct sun is best for germination. Check the soil every few days, keeping it always slightly moist.

Seed can take anywhere from 2 days to more than a month to germinate, and patience is required. After most of the seeds have germinated, remove the plastic, continuing to keep the young plants fairly moist. Transplant them to larger pots when they are crowded in the pot and large enough to handle.

Flowering of Cacti

Many cacti are grown for their flowers, others only for their spines or magnificent form. The likelihood of flowering varies enormously between species, with some cacti flowering only when they are very old, and others while still quite young. If your cacti don't bloom there could be any number of reasons why:

1. They are not growing vigorously enough during the year.
2. They are too shaded or cool or both.
3. They are receiving too much nitrogen fertilizer.
4. They are too young.
5. They are not receiving the proper periods of light and dark to trigger flowering.

If you are seriously interested in growing cacti for their flowers, there are two things to do:

1. Select a plant which flowers at a small size and doesn't need highly specialized conditions such as a very cold winter or a 100°F (38°C) summer. Many of the cacti and succulents listed in this book are noted as blooming easily indoors. A few of these are mammillaria, rebutia, gymnocalycium and kalanchoe. Choosing a plant which blooms readily indoors in the first place will solve half the problem.

2. Supply the proper conditions to encourage flowering. For many cacti (globe type in particular) a very dry and preferably cool winter rest period is essential for flowering. Keeping your cacti at around 50-55°F (10-13°C) and watering only when the soil becomes very dry will encourage flowering under home conditions.

Cactus and Succulent Problems

Cacti and succulents are as a whole relatively free of insects and diseases. Most problems are caused by poor growing practices such as insufficient lighting or over watering. Occasionally disorders may appear, however, and it is wise to be able to recognize their symptoms and apply a remedy.

Pest	Typical Damage	Control
MEALY BUGS	The nonmoving insects appear as cottony grey or white spots. Damage to a plant is through sucking juices, causing weakening of the plant and disfiguring of the new growth.	Squash or pick off insects individually. Touching the insects with a small paint brush dipped in alcohol will also destroy them.
ROOT MEALY BUGS	Ash-like deposits are seen on the roots of a plant during repotting. It will become generally unhealthy with no apparent cause, and may begin to rot.	Unpot plant and remove all soil from roots. Dip roots in a dilute solution of general purpose insecticide and repot in sterile soil. Systemic insecticides are also effective.
SPIDER MITES	Mites are very small and resemble dust. White speckling, and spider-like webbing between the spines are symptoms. Damage is by weakening of the plant through sucking plant juices.	Wash off every 5-7 days for 3 weeks with a strong stream of water, or spray at the same intervals with a miticide.
SCALE	Scale insects are immobile and appear as raised tan or brown dots on the body of a cactus or other succulent plant. The actual insects are hidden below the brown shell, where they suck plant juices causing weakening.	Scrape off individual insects as they appear. Systemic insecticides are also effective.
NEMATODES	Microscopic, wormlike animals living in the soil. They burrow into plant roots, causing swellings which keep the roots from functioning normally. The plant will become stunted and pale.	Unpot plant and remove all soil from the roots. Cut off all roots, let dry for several days and repot in sterile soil. A systemic insecticide is also effective.

Pest	Typical Damage	Control
APHIDS	Small soft-bodied insects with or without wings and in a variety of colors. They suck plant juices causing distorted growth.	Wash off with water or apply general purpose insecticide according to package directions.
SUNBURN	A plant receiving too much sun or being exposed to sun without being slowly conditioned to it will sunburn. The damage appears as yellowing or whitening of the leaves or body. Brown scabs may later form on the injured areas.	Remove plant from strong sunlight. Check care instructions for proper amount of light and adjust plant gradually to it.
LACK OF LIGHT	Insufficient light causes a plant to produce thin, weak new growth which is often long and scraggly looking.	Move plant to a more brightly lit area, adjusting it slowly to to the increased light.
ROT	An overwatered plant is most prone to rot, with the base becoming discolored and later soft and mushy. Examining the roots will show they are brown and decayed.	Cut off the rotted sections back to green healthy parts. Reroot the healthy parts if necessary.
CRESTING	See examples on pp. 18 and 56. A crest is produced when a growing tip develops abnormally, forming twisted and irregular growth. It is a mutation, but is considered very unique and attractive by some people. A crested plant may be weak and is often grown grafted for that reason.	Cresting does not harm a plant. It may begin spontaneously, and you may remove it or let it continue to develop as you choose.

To heighten your enjoyment and use of *Cacti and Succulents for Modern Living,* more than 100 full color photographs are shown in artistic settings. You can glean ideas for seasonal decoration as well as for year-round display.

You will find individual care instructions for each genus or plant group, including light and temperature requirements, watering, fertilization and soil needs, various uses, and how to make plants bloom. This detailed information, along with the general care instructions on Cacti and Succulents in the introductory section, is designed to make growing these flamboyant plants a joy instead of a chore. You will find both botanical and common name indexes, as well as helpful charts on problems and how to handle them.

Acknowledgements

Cacti and Succulents for Modern Living is a publication of Merchants Publishing Company, 20 Mills St., Kalamazoo, Michigan, quality printers for the horticultural industry.

Included photographs are from Merchants' library of horticultural subjects; a collection of over 15,000 color transparencies compiled by John C. Pike and the late Willard Kalina.

The text for *Cacti and Succulents for Modern Living* was written by Laura Williams Rice, M. Sc., horticultural specialist for Merchants Publishing Company. Guidance and assistance is acknowledged with thanks to Mary C. Bleck of Abbey Garden, Carpinteria, California.

We thank the following companies and individuals for their kind cooperation in providing assistance, materials, and some additional photographs for use in this book:

Abbey Garden, Mail Order Cactus and Succulent Nursery, Carpinteria, California; Anthony's Green Survival, Kalamazoo, Michigan; Atrium Candles and Plants, Kalamazoo, Michigan; Cacti Corner, Kalamazoo, Michigan; B.L. Cobia, Inc., Winter Garden, Florida; Desert Cactus, Kalamazoo, Michigan; Epiphyllum Society of America, P.O. Box 1395, Monrovia, California; Porter Featherstone, Newhall, California; Florida Cactus, Inc., Plymouth, Florida; Frank L. Geissler, Apopka, Florida; The Green Thumb, Kalamazoo, Michigan; Green Thumb Products, Apopka, Florida; Dr. M. Jane Coleman Helmer, Merchants Publishing Company; Michigan State University Horticulture Greenhouses, East Lansing, Michigan; Riverside Greenhouses, Kalamazoo, Michigan; Romence Garden and Trim Center, Kalamazoo, Michigan; Select Nurseries Inc., Brea, California; Bonnie E. Stewart, Merchants Publishing Company; Ed Storms, Fort Worth, Texas; University of Michigan, Matthi Botanical Gardens, Ann Arbor, Michigan; VanderSalms Flower Shop, Kalamazoo, Michigan; Walters Gardens, Inc., Zeeland, Michigan; Wildlife Plants Inc., Brighton, Michigan.

John Pike started his photographic career at the age of fifteen with a darkroom set up in his parents' basement. He has handled almost every area of photography from Chief Photographer for Civil Defense to photographing for *Motor Guide* magazine. John has been honored several times by professional photographers' associations. In the past few years he has travelled extensively for Merchants, photographing plants all over the United States.

Laura Williams Rice was educated at Ohio State and Michigan State Universities. Her interest in cacti and succulents grows from a tremendous enjoyment of all areas of horticulture. Laura has written articles and pamphlets on many plant-related subjects and currently writes a newspaper column on houseplants.

Living Rock *Ariocarpus fissuratus*

Truly resembling a rock, this unusual cactus requires careful treatment to live under household conditions.

Caring For Your Living Rock

Temperature: Average to warm in spring and summer (65-90°F, 19-32°C); cool (45-55°F, 7-13°C) in winter.

Light: Bright light.

Watering: Let soil approach dryness between waterings in spring and summer. Do not water at all from September through March; spray lightly only.

Fertilize: Every 2 months in spring and summer; none in winter.

Soil: A mixture of ⅔ coarse sand and ⅓ general houseplant soil. Plant only in a clay pot.

Additional Growing Information: Living Rocks will flower after reaching a diameter of 3" (8 cm). The dark pink flowers are produced in fall.

CACTI

STAR CACTUS
Astrophytum ornatum

Pronounced ribs are armed with radiating sets of amber spines. The body veiled in masses of felt-like spots, forming distinct patterns in age.

Caring For Your Star Cacti

Temperature: Average to warm (65-90°F,.19-32°C) in spring and summer; cool (45-55°F, 7-13°C) in fall and winter.

Light: Bright light.

Watering: Allow soil to approach dryness between waterings in spring and summer; keep quite dry in fall and winter.

Fertilize: Monthly spring through summer; none in winter.

Soil: A mixture of equal parts coarse sand and general houseplant soil.

Additional Growing Information: Star cacti will flower throughout the summer months when well grown. All species have yellow flowers.

SAND DOLLAR
Astrophytum asterias

Flattened cactus clearly creased around the body. Formally arranged wool buttons lend interest.

BISHOP'S CAP ▲
Astrophytum myriostigma

GOAT'S HORN ▶
Astrophytum capricorne v. minor
Grows to only 4 inches (10 cm) high,
bearing dwarf flowers.

Saguaro

Carnegiea gigantea
One of the slowest growing of all cacti.
A 10 year old plant may be only 6"
(15cm) high.

Caring For Your Saguaro

Temperature: Average to warm
(65-90°F, 19-32°C) in spring and
summer; cool (45-55°F, 7-13°C) in fall
and winter.

Light: Bright light.

Watering: Allow soil to approach dryness between waterings in spring and
summer; keep quite dry in fall and winter.

Fertilize: Every 2 months from spring
through summer; none in fall and winter.

Soil: A mixture of equal parts coarse
sand and general house plant soil.

Additional Growing Information:
Flowers should not be expected of
Saguaros since they will not be produced until the plant is about 5 feet
(1.5M) high.

Apple Cacti

CURIOSITY PLANT
*Cereus peruvianus
monstrose dwarf*

Slow growing mutation of Column Cactus. Forms very attractive spiney mounds.

Caring For Your Apple Cacti

Temperature: Average to warm (65-90°F, 19-32°C); cool (50-55°F, 10-13°C) in winter.

Light: Bright light all year is best, but will tolerate less light for some time if not actively growing.

Watering: Allow soil to approach dryness between waterings in spring and summer; keep very dry in fall and winter.

Fertilize: Every 2 months from spring through summer; none in winter.

Soil: A mixture of equal parts coarse sand and general house plant soil.

Additional Growing Information: The monstrose form of the normal Column Cactus pictured is a very hearty mutation and requires no special care to grow.

◄ COLUMN CACTUS
Cereus peruvianus

Tall, deeply ribbed cactus that is a favorite for interior decorating.

Silver Torch

Cleistocactus strausii

Caring For Your Silver Torch

Temperature: Average to warm (65-90°F, 19-32°C) in spring and summer; cool (50-55°F, 10-13°C) in winter.

Light: Bright light.

Watering: Let soil approach dryness between waterings in spring and summer. Keep quite dry in winter.

Fertilize: Monthly spring and summer.

Soil: A mixture of equal parts coarse sand and general house plant soil.

Additional Growing Information: Silver Torch will flower, but not until it reaches 5 ft. (1.5M). The red flowers are located along the sides of the plant.

Peanut Cactus *Chamaecereus silvestri*

Caring For Your Peanut Cactus

Temperature: Average to warm (65-90°F, 19-32°C) in spring and summer; cool (45-55°F, 7-13°C) in winter to encourage spring flowering.

Light: Bright light.

Watering: Allow soil to approach dryness between waterings in spring and summer; keep quite dry in fall and winter.

Fertilize: Monthly spring through summer; none in fall and winter.

Soil: A mixture of equal parts coarse sand and general house plant soil.

Additional Growing Information: Peanut Cacti will flower easily and profusely if given strong light and a long, cool dry period in winter.

Echinocactus grusonii

A traditionally favorite Barrel Cactus. Strong, straw yellow spines line each rib on older plants.

Caring For Your Golden Barrel

Temperature: Average to warm (65-90°F, 19-32°C) in spring and summer; cool (45-55°F, 7-13°C) in winter.

Light: Bright light.

Watering: Let soil approach dryness between waterings in spring and summer; keep quite dry in winter.

Fertilize: Monthly from spring through summer; none in fall and winter.

Soil: A mixture of equal parts coarse sand and general house plant soil.

Additional Growing Information: Grown for its lovely color. The yellow flowers will only be produced on plants over 12" (30cm) in diameter.

Golden Barrel

Elephant's Tooth

Coryphantha elephantidens

Slow growing Mammillaria relative with a characteristic lumpy texture.

Caring For Your Elephant's Tooth

Temperature: Average to warm 65-90°F, 19-32°C) in spring and summer; cool (45-50°F, 7-10°C) in fall and winter.

Light: Bright light.

Watering: Allow soil to approach dryness between waterings in spring and summer; keep quite dry in fall and winter.

Fertilize: Every 2 months from spring through summer. None in winter.

Soil: A mixture of ⅔ coarse sand and ⅓ general house plant soil.

Additional Growing Information: Many Coryphantha species naturally have a long tap root; they should be grown in fairly deep containers for proper root growth. Coryphanthas may be grown from seed.

RAINBOW CACTUS
Echinocereus v. neomexicanus

Forms tall columns with age, each banded with irregular stripes of pink and gold.

STRAWBERRY HEDGEHOG
Echinocereus engelmannii

Clustering brushland plant covered with dangerous looking long spines.

Hedgehog Cacti

Caring For Your Hedgehog Cactus

Temperature: Average to warm (65-90°F, 19-32°C) in spring and summer. Cool (45-55°F, 7-13°C) in winter to encourage flowering.

Light: Bright light.

Watering: Let soil approach dryness between waterings in spring and summer; keep quite dry in fall and winter.

Fertilize: Monthly from spring through summer. None in winter.

Soil: A mixture of equal parts coarse sand and general house plant soil.

Additional Growing Information: Cream Lace Cactus and Rainbow Cactus will flower when only 3" (8cm) high when given a cool, dry dormant period in winter. Strawberry Hedgehogs must be larger and older before flowering will start.

CREAM LACE CACTUS
Echinocereus reichenbachii v. fitchii

Easily grown cactus with brilliantly colored flowers lasting several days.

Brain Cactus *Echinofossulocactus species*

An easy-to-grow cactus with zigzaging ribs running down the body.

Caring For Your Echinofossulocactus

Temperature: Average to warm (65-90°F, 19-32°C) in spring and summer. Cool (45-55°F, 7-13°C) in winter.

Light: Bright light.

Watering: Let soil approach dryness in between waterings spring and summer; allow to become quite dry between waterings in winter.

Fertilize: Monthly spring through summer. None in fall and winter.

Soil: A mixture of equal parts coarse sand and general house plant soil.

Additional Growing Information: Echinofossulocactus flowers easily at a young age after a cool, dry winter rest. The blossoms may be pink, purple, or white.

Echinopsis 'Haku Jo' ▶

Unusual appearing Echinopsis with strongly pronounced ribs and rust colored spines.

Haku Jo

Caring For Your Haku Jo

Temperature: Average to warm (65-90°F, 19-32°C) in spring and summer; cool (45-55°F, 7-13°C) in winter.

Light: Bright light for best growth, though will live with only moderate light.

Watering: Let soil approach dryness between waterings in spring and summer; keep quite dry in fall and winter.

Fertilize: Monthly spring through summer. None in winter.

Soil: A mixture of equal parts coarse sand and general house plant soil.

Additional Growing Information: Echinopsis cacti flower readily, producing large pink or white blooms throughout the summer.

Epiphyllums

Caring For Your Epiphyllums

Temperature: Average to warm (65-100°F, 19-38°C), in spring and summer; cool, down to a minimum of 41°F (5°C) in winter.

Light: Moderate light. Should receive some sunshine, but not full sun all day.

Watering: Although Epiphyllums are succulent and tolerant of drought, they will grow best if the soil is kept slightly moist. Do not use very alkaline water as Epiphyllums grow best under acid conditions.

Fertilize: Monthly from early spring through fall with a low nitrogen, acid type fertilizer. Do not fertilize in winter.

Soil: A humusy houseplant soil well supplied with leaf mold and a little horticultural charcoal.

Additional Growing Information:
Epiphyllums bloom throughout the year depending on the particular variety. Propagation is by cuttings taken from a mature branch of a mother plant. Allow the cuttings to dry for 2 weeks before planting in barely moist soil. Withhold water for at least 3 weeks, then gradually start watering normally.

Epiphyllum hybrid ▼

Epiphyllum 'Showboat' ▲

Occasionally called Orchid Cacti because of their spectacular blossoms, Epiphyllums make graceful and attractive hanging basket plants even without blooms.

Epiphyllum 'Paul de Longpre' ▲

The named varieties of Epiphyllums are too numerous to mention, and it is nearly impossible to distinguish between them without the blooms being present.

Peruvian Old Man *Espostoa lanata*

Easy-to-grow plant completely covered with striking white hair.

Caring For Your Peruvian Old Man

Temperature: Average to warm (65-90°F, 19-32°C) in spring and summer; cool (45-55°F, 7-13°C) in fall and winter.

Light: Bright light.

Watering: Allow soil to approach dryness between waterings in spring and summer; keep quite dry in fall and winter.

Fertilize: Monthly from spring through fall. None in winter.

Soil: A mixture of equal parts coarse sand and general houseplant soil.

Additional Growing Information: All hairy type cacti such as Espostoa, Oreocereus and Cephalocereus require very strong light for good growth, since the hair partially screens out light.

Fire Barrel

Ferocactus acanthodes

Brilliant red, hooked spines characterize this protected species of barrel cactus.

Caring For Your Fire Barrel

Temperature: Average to warm (65-90°F, 19-32°C) in spring and summer. Cool (45-55°F, 7-13°C) during the winter rest period.

Light: Bright light.

Watering: Let soil approach dryness between waterings in spring and summer. Keep quite dry in fall and winter.

Fertilize: Every 2 months from spring until fall. None in winter.

Soil: A mixture of equal parts coarse sand and general houseplant soil.

Additional Growing Information: Barrel Cacti, both Ferocactus and Echinocactus, are slow growing and need strong light to keep their attractive rounded shape.

ROSE-PLAID CACTUS
Gymnocalycium mihanovichii friedrichii

A profuse bloomer, literally covering itself with delicate pink blossoms.

DWARF CHIN CACTI
Gymnocalycium quehlianum and Gymnocalycium baldianum

Curious, protruding "chins" under each radiating set of spines are the mark of Gymnocalycium cacti.

Chin Cacti

Caring For Your Chin Cactus

Temperature: Average to warm (65-90°F, 19-32°C) in spring and summer; cool (50-55°F, 10-13°C) in fall and winter to encourage flowering.

Light: Bright to moderate light.

Watering: Let soil approach dryness between waterings in spring and summer; keep quite dry in fall and winter.

Fertilize: Monthly from spring through fall.

Soil: A mixture of equal parts coarse sand and general house plant soil.

Additional Growing Information:
Chin Cacti are among the easiest cacti to flower under home conditions, producing large numbers of flowers when still very young. They are propagated from seed or by separating individual plants from larger clusters.

BRUCH'S CHIN CACTUS
Gymnocalycium bruchii

Delicate appearing, clustering plant with tiny beige spines.

Devil's Head

Homalocephala texensis

The only plant in its genus, Devil's Head is a very sturdy plant, closely related to Barrel Cacti (Echinocactus and Ferocactus).

Caring For Your Devil's Head

Temperature: Average to warm (65-90°F, 19-32°C) in spring and summer, cool (45-55°F, 7-13°C) in winter.

Light: Bright light.

Watering: Let soil approach dryness between waterings in spring and summer while growing. Keep quite dry in fall and winter.

Soil: A mixture of equal parts coarse sand and general house plant soil.

Fertilize: Every 2 months from spring through summer only. None in winter.

Additional Growing Information: The flowers of Devil's Head last for several days and are fragrant. The pink seed pods which are formed later are decorative for several months.

Agave Cactus

Leuchtenbergia principis

Agave Cactus is the only plant in the genus Leuchtenbergia. The attractive, large yellow flowers are produced at the base of the plant.

Caring For Your Agave Cactus

Temperature: Average (65-80°F, 19-27°C) all year.

Light: Bright light.

Watering: Let soil approach dryness in spring and summer; keep quite dry in fall and winter.

Fertilize: Monthly from spring through summer. None in winter.

Soil: A mixture of equal parts coarse sand and general house plant soil.

Additional Growing Information: Agave Cacti have long tap roots and will grow best in deep pots which will allow the roots to develop normally. Propagate by seed.

Montrose Totem Pole

*Lophocereus schottii
monstrosus*

This montrose variety of Lophocereus is highly attractive with its
lumpy texture and complete lack
of spines.

Caring For Your
Montrose Totem Pole

Temperature: Average to warm
(65-90°F, 19-32°C) in spring and
summer; cool (45-55°F, 7-13°C)
in fall and winter.

Light: Bright Light.

Watering: Let soil approach dryness
between waterings in the spring and
summer growing period; allow to
dry well between waterings in winter.

Fertilize: Every month from spring
through summer. None in winter.

Soil: A mixture of equal parts coarse
sand and general house plant soil.

Additional Growing Information:
Montrose Totem Pole is grown for
its interesting shape. Flowers are
seldom produced.

Pincushion Cacti

◀ OWL'S EYES
Mammillaria parkinsonii

Snowy white spines interlace around each rounded cactus body. Large clusters form with age.

OLD LADY CACTUS
Mammillaria hahniana

Winter flowering cactus with reddish purple blossoms opening over the silky-haired body.

POWDER PUFF
Mammillaria bocasana

Produces apricot blossoms ½" across.

Mammillaria polyedra ▲

An interesting cactus dense-ly studded with knobby areoles.

BIRDSNEST CACTUS ▲
Mammillaria camptotricha:

Small white flowers are borne among the curved yellow spines.

Caring For Your Mammillaria

Temperature: Average to warm (65-90°F, 19-32°C) in spring and summer; cool (45-55°F, 7-13°C) in winter to encourage flowering.

Light: Bright light. The strongest light is required for extremely spiny or hairy types since much light is screened from reaching the body of the cactus.

Watering: Let soil approach dryness between waterings in spring and summer. Keep quite dry in fall and winter while resting.

Fertilize: Monthly spring through summer; none in winter.

Soil: A mixture of equal parts coarse sand and general house plant soil.

Additional Growing Information:
Pincushions are probably the most common type of cactus grown indoors. They are generally easily grown, flower readily when young and many form large clusters with age. They are recognized by the ring-like pattern in which they bear their flowers.

SNOWBALL PINCUSHION ▶
Mammillaria candida v. caespitosa

This Pincushion can be prone to rot and should be watched and watered carefully.

29

FEATHER CACTUS
Mammillaria plumosa

Unique cactus with plumes for spines. Rarely flowers, but can produce greenish white blooms in December.

GOLDEN STARS ▼
Mammillaria elongata

A common indoor cactus, forming long finger-like branches and showing small white flowers in spring.

RAINBOW PINCUSHION
Mammillaria rhodantha

An easy to grow species, attractive all year with its brightly colored spines. Mid-summer flowers are deep red.

Caring For Your Mammillaria:
See Page 29.

DWARF TURK'S CAP ▶
Melocactus matazanus:

Forms its "cephalium" or bristly cap at a young age (4 years), and may flower indoors in winter at that time.

Turk's Cap

Caring For Your Turk's Cap

Temperature: Average to warm all year (65-90°F, 19-32°C) with a minimum winter temperature of 60°F (15°C).

Light: Moderate to bright light.

Watering: Allow soil to approach dryness between waterings all year. Do not let soil dry excessively in winter.

Fertilize: Monthly from spring through summer. None in winter.

Soil: A mixture of equal parts coarse sand and general house plant soil.

Additional Growing Information: Turk's Caps are among the best cacti to grow indoors, requiring less strong sun than most types and no cool, dry dormant period. Grows well under lights.

TURK'S CAP
Melocactus obtusipetalus:

This Turk's Cap takes many years to mature and develop a "cap". It will not increase in size after the cap is formed.

Neoporteria

Neoporteria gerocephala

A lovely rose flowered Neoporteria with beige-brown spines.

Caring For Your Neoporteria

Temperature: Average to warm (65-90°F, 19-32°C) all year.

Light: Bright Light.

Watering: Allow soil to dry well between waterings all year.

Fertilize: Monthly from spring through fall. None in winter.

Soil: A mixture of equal parts coarse sand and general house plant soil.

Additional Growing Information: Neoporteria Cacti are prone to rotting problems and should always be watered sparingly. Flowers are produced readily in mid-fall and may be pink, yellow, purple, or white.

Ball Cacti

◀ SUN CAP
Notocactus apricus

Sparsely spined notocactus with buttercup yellow flowers.

GOLDEN BALL ▶
Notocactus leninghausii

Rich golden-spined Ball Cactus with yellow blossoms.

SILVER BALL
Notocactus scopa

Fragile, silky spined plant with yellow flowers in spring.

Caring For Your Ball Cacti

Temperature: Average to warm (65-90°F, 19-32°C) in spring and summer, cool (50-55°F, 10-13°C) in winter.

Light: Bright light.

Watering: Let soil approach dryness between waterings in spring and summer. Keep quite dry in fall and winter.

Fertilize: Monthly spring through summer. None in winter.

Soil: A mixture of equal parts coarse sand and general house plant soil.

Additional Growing Information: Notocacti are easy-to-grow cacti, and many flower at a young age.

SCARLET BALL
Notocactus haselbergii

Unique red flowered Ball Cactus.

Artichoke Cactus

Obregonia denegrii

Caring for Your Artichoke Cactus

Temperature: Average to warm (65-90°F, 19-32°C) in spring and summer, cool (50-55°F, 10-13°C) in winter.

Light: Bright light.

Watering: Let soil approach dryness between waterings in spring and summer. Allow to dry thoroughly between waterings in winter.

Fertilizer: Monthly in spring and summer. None in winter.

Soil: A mixture of equal parts coarse sand and general house plant soil.

Additional Growing Information: Can be grown from seed, although it is a very slow grower. Seldom flowers indoors.

Opuntia

PAPER SPINE
Opuntia paediophylla

Caring For Your Opuntia

Temperature: Average to warm (65-90°F, 19-32°C) in spring and summer, cool (45-55°F, 7-13°C) in winter.

Light: Bright light.

Watering: Let soil approach dryness between waterings in spring and summer. Let soil dry well between waterings in winter, but beware of over drying which may cause pads to drop on some varieties.

Fertilize: Monthly from spring through fall. None in winter.

Soil: A mixture of equal parts coarse sand and general house plant soil.

Additional Growing Information: Most Opuntias are rapid growing and require a large amount of root room. They usually do not flower indoors and may be propagated easily by rooting single pads or sections of several pads. Most of them have small clusters of spines called glochids which appear as dots on the pads. The spines embed in the skin on contact and are very irritating.

CINNAMON CACTUS
Opuntia rufida

BLACK-SPINED PRICKLY PEAR
Opuntia violacea

EVE'S PIN CACTUS
Opuntia sublata

BUNNY EARS
Opuntia microdasys

Old Man of the Andes

OLD MAN OF THE ANDES
Oreocereus celsianus:

Beware of the sharp yellow-brown spines beneath the silvery hair of this Old Man cactus.

Caring For Your Old Man of the Andes

Temperature: Average to warm (65-90°F, 19-32°C) during spring and summer; cool (45-55°F, 7-13°C) during fall and winter.

Light: Bright light is essential since the silky hairs screen out a great deal of sun.

Watering: Allow soil to approach dryness in spring and summer; keep quite dry in winter.

Fertilize: Every 2 months from spring through summer. None in winter.

Soil: A mixture of equal parts coarse sand and general house plant soil.

Additional Growing Information: The hairiness of Old Man Cacti is due partially to the intensity of the sunlight which the plant receives. If your plant lacks thick hair, it may be because the natural light in your climate is not strong enough.

OLD MAN OF THE ANDES
Oreocereus trollii:

A slow growing, hair covered cactus appearing almost rounded when young but becoming more column shaped with age.

Barbados Gooseberry

Pereskia aculeata

Caring For Your Pereskia

Temperature: Average to warm (50-85°F, 10-30°C) all year.

Light: Moderate to bright light.

Watering: Keep soil moist in spring and summer, but allow soil to dry between waterings in winter.

Fertilize: Monthly from spring through fall. None in winter.

Soil: Any general house plant mix.

Additional Growing Information:
The leafy type growth of Pereskia influences its care, and it should be treated more as a foliage plant than a cactus. Be sure to allow plenty of room for root growth, and watch out for sharp spines hidden beneath the leaves.

Woolly Torch *Pilosocereus maxonii*

Extremely beautiful and sturdy cactus, azure blue and irregularly thatched with shaggy champagne colored hair.

Caring For Your Woolly Torch

Temperature: Average to warm (65-90°F, 19-32°C) all year.

Light: Bright light.

Watering: Allow soil to approach dryness between waterings in spring and summer. Keep quite dry in fall and winter.

Fertilize: Every two months while growing throughout spring and summer. None in fall and winter.

Soil: A mixture of equal parts coarse sand and general house plant soil.

Additional Growing Information:
The attractive mane on Woolly Torch can be cleaned by gentle shampooing with any detergent and water, although some discoloration may result.

Crown Cacti

Caring for Your Crown Cactus

Temperature: Average to warm (65-90°F, 19-32°C) cool (45-55°F, 7-13°C) in winter.

Light: Moderate light. Do not place in full sun when growing outdoors.

Watering: Let soil approach dryness in spring and summer. Allow soil to dry well between waterings in winter to promote bud formation.

Fertilize: Monthly spring through summer. None in winter.

Soil: A mixture of equal parts coarse sand and general houseplant soil.

Additional Growing Information: Rebutias bloom readily and produce their flowers around the base of the plant in spring.

Rebutia senilis hybrid

SUN REBUTIA
Rebutia heliosa

CROWN CACTUS
Rebutia krainziana

Easter Cacti

▲ **SCARLET EASTER CACTUS**
Rhipsalidopsis cv. 'Andrae'

Caring For Your Easter Cactus

Temperature: Average to warm (65-90°F, 19-32°C) in spring and summer; cool (45-55°F, 7-13°C) in fall and winter to encourage flower bud formation.

Light: Moderate light. Avoid long periods of strong direct sunlight.

Watering: Keep soil moist throughout most of the year, but allow to approach dryness in fall and winter to encourage flower buds to form. Resume keeping soil moist when buds first appear.

Fertilize: Monthly only from after blooming until late summer.

Soil: Any general house plant soil.

Additional Growing Information:

Easter Cactus blooms naturally in the spring. To flower, it must have a combination of cold, drought and short daylength. Gradually reduce the watering frequency in late August for 8-12 weeks and do not fertilize. Place the cactus where it will receive cool night temperatures (down to 40°F, 5°C), and at least 13 hours of **continuous** darkness nightly. After the buds form, your Easter Cactus may be returned to normal indoor conditions where the buds will open.

ROSE EASTER CACTUS ▶
Rhipsalidopsis rosea

39

Christmas Cacti

WHITE CHRISTMAS ▶
Zygocactus truncatus 'Alba' (Pat. 3574)
Attractive white Christmas Cactus variety ideal for holiday decoration.

◀ CHRISTMAS CHEER
Zygocactus truncatus 'Christmas Cheer'
Produces bright red blooms in great numbers from November through January.

Caring For Your Christmas Cactus

Temperature: Average to warm (65-90°F, 19-32°C) most of the year; cool (45-55°F, 7-13°C) in fall to aid in flower bud formation.

Light: Moderate light. Long periods of strong, direct sunlight will cause sunburn.

Watering: Keep soil moist from when buds appear (October or November) through summer. Keep drier beginning in September for bud formation.

Fertilize: Monthly from after blooming through summer; none in fall and winter.

Soil: Any general house plant soil.

Additional Growing Information: Christmas Cactus has recently been put into the genus Schlumbergera whose members are very similar in appearance. It can no longer correctly be called Zygocactus.

To flower for Christmas, these cacti must have cool temperatures, drier soil, and the naturally shorter days of fall. If a plant receives artificial lighting at night, it probably will not flower, so you may wish to enclose your plant in a closet each night or in an unused room. Do this from early September until the buds are showing, decreasing the watering at the same time.

Dropping of unopened flower buds is a common problem on Christmas Cactus. It may be caused by any of several reasons: a sudden rise or fall in temperature, change in light intensity or direction or simply that the plant is producing more blossoms than it can support.

Grafted Cacti

Caring For Your Grafted Cacti

Temperature: Average to warm (65-90°F, 19-32°C) in spring and summer; cooler in winter (50-55°F, 10-13°C).

Light: Bright light.

Watering: Allow soil to approach dryness between waterings in spring and summer; keep drier in winter.

Fertilize: Monthly from spring through summer; none in winter.

Soil: A mixture of equal parts coarse sand and general houseplant soil.

Additional Growing Information: Cacti are usually grafted because the top plant (scion) is a weak grower on its own natural roots. Grafting it onto a vigorous growing base (stock) will make the scion healthier and faster growing.

GRAFTED CACTI

Interesting combinations of 2 different cacti, grafted cacti are increasingly popular novelty plants.

CALICO HEARTS
Adromischus rupicolus
Produces decoratively speckled leaves the size of half dollars.

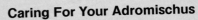

Caring For Your Adromischus

Temperature: Average to warm (65-90°F, 19-32°C) all year.

Light: Moderate light.

Watering: Allow soil to approach dryness between waterings in spring and summer; maintain quite dry in fall and winter.

Fertilize: Monthly while actively growing; none in winter.

Soil: A mixture of equal parts coarse sand and general houseplant soil.

Additional Growing Information: Easily propagated by individual leaves laid on the soil.

PLOVER EGGS
Adromischus cooperi
Small, easy-to-grow succulent which does not require long periods of direct sunlight.

Aeonium

COPPER PINWHEEL
Aeonium decorum

Caring For Your Aeonium

Temperature: Average (65-90°F, 19-32°C) all year.

Light: Bright light.

Watering: When growing, water well and then allow soil to approach dryness before watering again. Let soil dry well between waterings when dormant.

Fertilize: Monthly while actively growing; none while dormant.

Soil: A combination of equal parts coarse sand and general houseplant soil.

Additional Growing Information:
Aeoniums grow during the winter in nature, but may switch to become summer growing indoors. You can determine which growing cycle your Aeonium is in by watching for the signs of dormancy: a closing and shrinking of the leafy rosette.

Flowering usually occurs in late winter or spring. The mature rosette will die after-wards, being replaced by sucker shoots which grow from the base.

BLACK TREE ▼
Aeonium arboreum var. atropurpureum

GIANT VELVET ROSE
Aeonium canariense

43

Agave

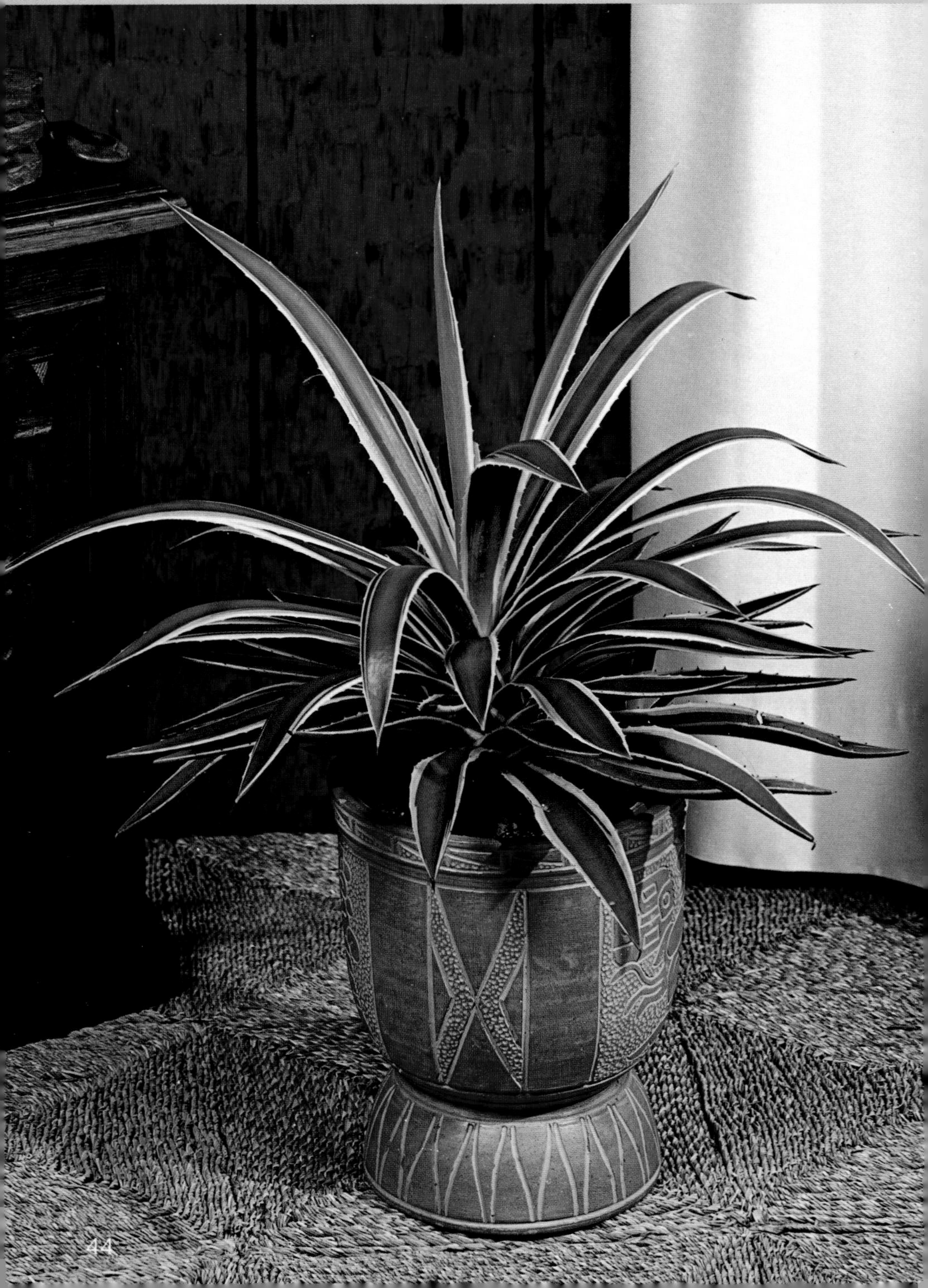

Caring For Your Agave

Temperature: Average to warm (65-90°F, 19-32°C) all year.

Light: Bright light is preferable; some species will tolerate reduced light intensities for extended periods.

Watering: Allow soil to approach dryness between waterings when growing in spring and summer. Water less often in winter.

Fertilize: Monthly from spring through summer; none in winter.

Soil: A mixture of equal parts coarse sand and general houseplant soil.

Additional Growing Information: May be propagated by breaking off and rooting suckers which appear at the base of large plants.

◀ QUEEN AGAVE
Agave victoriae-reginae

Sturdy leaves are attractively channeled, and edged with delicate white lines.

Agave univittata ▼

Deep green agave contrastingly marked in paler green down the center of each leaf.

VARIEGATED CARIBBEAN AGAVE
Agave angustifolia cv. marginata

A common variety with sharply toothed white leaf edges.

45

PARTRIDGE BREAST ALOE
Aloe variegata

Dwarf, beautifully marked aloe perfect for window-sill growing.

GOLDTOOTH ALOE
Aloe mitriformis

Large, thick-leaved aloe with many sharp teeth along the leaf edges.

MEDICINAL ALOE
Aloe barbadensis (vera)

The mucilage-like sap has been used for centuries in treating burns and cuts.

Caring For Your Aloe

Temperature: Average to warm (65-90°F, 19-32°C) all year.

Light: Bright light.

Watering: Let soil approach dryness between waterings in spring and summer; keep drier in fall and winter.

Fertilize: Monthly from spring through summer; none in winter.

Soil: A mixture of equal parts coarse sand and general houseplant soil.

Additional Growing Information:
Propagated from suckers which develop at the base of large plants.

CANDELABRA ALOE
Aloe arborescens

This aloe has a distinctly upright stem, with the leaves widely spaced and forming the arms of the "candelabra".

Pony Tail Palm *Beaucarnea recurvata*

An adaptable plant which will eventually grow into a 20 foot (6M) tree if given room.

Caring For Your Pony Tail Palm

Temperature: Average to warm (65-90°F, 19-32°C) all year.

Light: Moderate to bright light.

Watering: Allow soil to dry partially between waterings.

Fertilize: Monthly while actively growing.

Soil: Any general houseplant soil that drains well.

Additional Growing Information: Pony Tail Palm is considered to be a succulent because of the unusual swollen base which contains stored water; this can sustain the plant during long periods of drought.

48

Climbing Onion

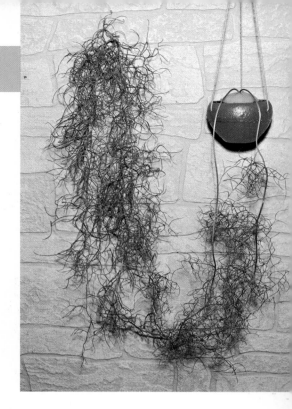

Bowiea volubilis

Caring For Your Climbing Onion

Temperature: Average to warm (65-90°F, 19-32°C) all year.

Light: Moderate to bright light.

Watering: Allow soil to dry partially between waterings when the plant is actively growing. Do not water during dormant period.

Fertilize: Monthly while actively growing; none while dormant.

Soil: Any general houseplant soil which drains well.

Additional Growing Information:
Climbing Onion is naturally winter growing with a dormant period during the summer. As summer approaches, gradually reduce watering frequency and amount of water given. The foliage will die back and the bulb will become dormant. Do not water at all after this, but resume regular watering in fall.

Cone Plant *Conophytum meyeri*

Caring For Your Cone Plant

Temperature: Average to warm (65-90°F, 19-32°C) all year.

Light: Bright light.

Watering: Allow soil to dry completely between infrequent light waterings (about every 3 weeks) during the dormant period (approximately June through August). Give frequent light waterings during the balance of the year, but always allow soil to approach dryness between waterings.

Fertilize: Monthly during the growing season; none while dormant.

Soil: A mixture of 2/3 coarse sand and 1/3 general houseplant soil.

Additional Growing Information:
Cone Plants naturally grow during the winter, but may switch over to a summer growing schedule in cultivation. They are propagated from seed or cuttings.

Cotyledon

◄ **SCARLET BELLS**
Cotyledon macrantha

Large, 6″ (15 cm) diameter leaves form the loose, fleshy rosette.

Cotyledons naturally grow during the winter, but may switch over to a summer growing schedule in cultivation.

Caring For Your Cotyledon

Temperature: Average to warm (65-90°F, 19-32°C) all year.

Light: Bright light.

Watering: Allow soil to approach dryness between waterings while actively growing (usually fall and winter.) Water sparingly and less frequently during July and August.

Fertilize: Monthly while actively growing. None while dormant.

Soil: A mixture of equal parts coarse sand and general houseplant soil.

Additional Growing Information: The beautiful, bell-like flowers are produced in spring or summer. Propagate from cuttings.

CORAL BELLS
Cotyledon orbiculata

Apple-green leaves masked with silver beneath.

50

Jade Plants

JADE PLANT
Crassula portulacea (argentea)

A common and widely known household succulent.

MINIATURE JADE PLANT
Crassula portulacea minima

Dwarf-leaved Jade Plant with tiny ½" (1.5 cm) leaves on a normal sized plant.

Caring For Your Jade Plant

Temperature: Average to warm (65-90°F, 19-32°C) all year.

Light: Bright light; strong light is especially necessary for variegated types.

Watering: Allow soil to dry between waterings.

Fertilize: Monthly while growing rapidly in spring and summer; none in fall and winter unless growth continues and light is strong.

Soil: A combination of equal parts coarse sand and general houseplant soil.

Additional Growing Information: Jade Plants root easily and form new plants from single leaves laid on the soil.

TRICOLOR JADE
VARIEGATED JADE PLANT ▶
Crassula portulacea 'Tricolor Jade'

Beautiful variegated version of the regular Jade Plant. Leaf edges turn pink in strong sun.

Caring For Your Crassula

Temperature: Average to warm (65-90°F, 19-32°C) all year.

Light: Bright light.

Watering: Allow soil to dry between waterings.

Fertlilze: Monthly while growing in spring and summer, none in winter unless growth continues and light is strong.

Soil: A combination of equal parts coarse sand and general houseplant soil.

Additional Growing Information: Crassulas can be easily propagated from cuttings.

◀ PRINCESS PINE
Crassula lycopodioides

A creeping crassula which looks well in a hanging basket.

PROPELLER PLANT
Crassula falcata

Bears bright red flowers in summer, giving it the common name of Scarlet Paintbrush.

NECKLACE VINE ▶
Crassula perforata

53

ECHEVERIA
Echeveria pubescens

White, velvety hair gives this Echeveria a glistening appearance.

ECHEVERIA
Echeveria hybrid

A spring flowerer with numerous spikes of golden bell-like flowers.

Echeveria

Caring For Your Echeveria

Temperature: Average to warm (65-90°F, 19-32°C) in spring and summer; cool (50-55°F, 10-13°C) in winter.

Light: Bright light.

Watering: Let soil approach dryness between waterings in spring and summer; keep drier in fall and winter.

Fertilize: Monthly in spring and summer; none in winter.

Soil: A mixture of equal parts coarse sand and general houseplant soil.

Additional Growing Information:
Excellent patio plants for planting in strawberry jars. Propagate by removing and rooting small "chicks" which form on mature plants of many species, or by rooting leaves.

ECHEVERIA
Echeveria dactylifera

Red rimming of the leaves creates an interesting effect.

Crown of Thorns

GIANT CROWN OF THORNS
Euphorbia hybrid
  (lophogona x milii v. Splendens)

Large-leaved hybrid variety.

Caring For Your Crown of Thorns

Temperature: Warm (70°F, 21°C and up all year).

Light: Bright light. Will tolerate less light, but may not bloom as well.

Watering: Allow soil to become slightly dry between waterings. Too dry soil will cause the leaves to drop.

Fertilize: Monthly from early spring through summer; none in winter.

Soil: A mixture of equal parts coarse sand and general houseplant soil

Additional Growing Information: Crown of Thorns bloom sporadically throughout the year. They are propagated from cuttings.

CROWN OF THORNS
Euphorbia milii v. splendens

Traditional favorite, though it becomes quite rambling with age.

◀ CANDELABRA EUPHORBIA
Euphorbia lactea

Strong, curving branches attractively decorated with pale green banding.

AFRICAN MILK TREE ▶
Euphorbia trigona

Appropriately named for the milky sap which oozes from the plant when injured.

Euphorbia

Caring For Your Euphorbia

Temperature: Average to warm (65-90°F, 19-32°C) all year.

Light: Bright light, though some species will grow in only moderate light.

Watering: Allow soil to approach dryness between waterings.

Fertilize: Monthly from spring through fall.

Soil: A mixture of equal parts coarse sand and general houseplant soil.

Additional Growing Information:
All members of this plant family, including Poinsettia and Crown of Thorns ooze a milky sap when the leaves or stems are damaged. The sap can be irritating to the skin, and should be washed off immediately.

◀ CRESTED COW'S HORN
Euphorbia grandicornis
cv. cristata

A popular crested Euphorbia almost antler-like in shape.

Euphorbia cereiformis ▲

Stubby, red spines line each of the closely set ribs.

PENCIL EUPHORBIA ▼
Euphorbia tirucalli

Pencil-thick angular branches tipped in spring with tiny yellow flowers.

MEDUSA'S HEAD
Euphorbia pugniformis

Flat growing succulent with many slender, nubby branches.

Tiger Jaws

Faucaria hybrid

Caring For Your Tiger Jaws

Temperature: Average to warm (65-90°F, 19-32°C) all year.

Light: Bright light.

Watering: Allow soil to approach dryness between waterings for most of the year. Water less frequently and more lightly in summer when the plant is semi-dormant (after blooming).

Fertilize: Monthly during the growing period; none while dormant.

Soil: A mixture of 2/3 coarse sand and 1/3 general houseplant soil.

Additional Growing Information: Tiger Jaws are naturally winter growing, but may switch over to summer growing in cultivation.

Baby Toes

Fenestraria rhopalophylla

Caring For Your Baby Toes

Temperature: Average to warm (65-90°F, 19-32°C) all year.

Light: Bright light.

Watering: Allow soil to dry completely between infrequent, light waterings (about every 2 weeks) during the dormant period: approximately June through August. Give frequent, light waterings the balance of the year, but allow soil to approach dryness between each watering.

Fertilize: Monthly during the growing period; none while dormant.

Soil: A combination of 2/3 coarse sand and 1/3 general houseplant soil.

Additional Growing Information: Under their normal growing conditions, Baby Toes grow submerged in the soil to their tops, with only their transparent windows exposed. However, when growing them as houseplants, Baby Toes must be grown with the stems above the soil to avoid rot problems.

Baby Toes naturally grow during the winter, but may switch over to a summer growing schedule in cultivation.

Ox Tongue *Gasteria hybrid*

The straplike leaves of Ox Tongue are leathery and frequently adorned with horny warts.

Caring For Your Ox Tongue

Temperature: Average to warm (65-90°F, 19-32°C) all year.

Light: Moderate light.

Watering: Allow soil to approach dryness between waterings.

Fertilize: Every 2 months during spring and summer; none in winter.

Soil: A mixture of equal parts coarse sand and general houseplant soil.

Additional Growing Information: Ox Tongue will grow year round in most homes. It may be propagated from small sucker plants growing from the base of larger plants or by rooting single leaves.

Ghost Plant *Graptopetalum paraguayense*

A cascading jumble of silver-blue rosettes.

Caring For Your Ghost Plant

Temperature: Average to warm (65-90°F, 19-32°C) in spring and summer; cool (50-55°F, 10-13°C) in fall and winter.

Light: Bright light.

Watering: Let soil approach dryness in spring and summer; keep drier in fall and winter.

Fertilize: Monthly in spring and summer; none in winter.

Soil: A mixture of equal parts coarse sand and general houseplant soil.

Additional Growing Information: Excellent patio plant suited to growing in hanging baskets. Propagate by cuttings.

59

Irish Rose

Greenovia dodrentalis (gracilis)

Caring For Your Irish Rose

Temperature: Average to warm (65-90°F, 19-32°C) all year.

Light: Moderate light.

Watering: Allow soil to approach dryness between waterings when in growth; water less frequently when dormant.

Fertilize: Monthly while growing, none while dormant.

Soil: A mixture of equal parts coarse sand and general houseplant soil.

Additional Growing Information: Irish Rose grows in winter in nature, but may switch to become summer growing in cultivation. The rosettes will close up and appear smaller when the plant is dormant, and it should be watered less frequently at this time.

Propagate from small plants produced by the mother plant during the growing season.

Haworthia

◀ **LITTLE ZEBRA PLANT**
Haworthia subfasciata

The most commonly known Haworthia; a windowsill favorite.

Caring For Your Haworthia

Temperature: Average to warm (65-90°F, 19-32°C) all year.

Light: Moderate light. Avoid excessive periods of direct sun.

Watering: Allow soil to approach dryness between waterings.

Fertilize: Once in spring and once in fall. Avoid summer fertilization while the plant is in a short rest period.

Soil: A mixture of equal parts coarse sand and general houseplant soil.

Additional Growing Information: Haworthias are extremely sturdy plants which do not require as much light as most other succulents. They are propagated by offsets formed at the base of larger plants.

◀ *Haworthia mucronata*

Bears almost transparent, pale green leaves, and is less warty than other Haworthias.

Haworthia hybrid ▲

Smooth green leaves spring bowtie fashion from the growing center.

◀ FAIRY WASHBOARD
Haworthia limifolia

A deep green rosette of swirling leaves.

Wax Plants

◀ **LURA-LEI**
Hoya carnosa compacta
'Mauna Loa'
(Pat. 3054)

KRIMSON PRINCESS® ◀
Hoya carnosa rubra
(Pat. 3105)

Caring For Your Wax Plant

Temperature: Average to warm (65-90°F, 19-32°C) all year.

Light: Moderate light. Strong, direct sun will injure the plant.

Watering: Allow soil to dry partially between waterings.

Fertilize: Monthly in spring, summer, and fall while actively growing; none during the winter months of December, January, and February.

Soil: A mixture of equal parts coarse sand and general houseplant soil.

Additional Growing Information: Wax Plants are propagated by cuttings. The leafless stalks form the flower clusters each year and should not be removed. Your Wax Plant will flower best if potbound.

Cockleburs *Huernia hybrid (pillansii x macrocarpa)*

...assing plant with individual "Cockleburs" only 3" (7.6 cm) high.

aring For Your Cockleburs

emperature: Average to warm (65-90°F, 19-32°C) all year.

ight: Bright light.

atering: Allow soil to dry well between waterings.

ertilize: Monthly in spring and summer while actively growing.

oil: A combination of equal parts coarse sand and general houseplant soil.

dditional Growing Information: Propagated by dividing clumps or rooting cuttings **a**ken when actively growing.

Flowering Kalanchoes

Kalanchoe 'Fuerball'

The ever popular Kalanchoe of the florist trade; these succulents have long lasting flowers in a wide array of colors including red, pink, yellow, and apricot.

Kalanchoe manginii

Delicate Kalanchoe with dime sized leaves and pendulous coral blooms. Cascading stems make it suited to hanging baskets.

Caring For Your Flowering Kalanchoe

Temperature: Average to warm (65-90°F, 19-32°C) all year.

Light: Bright light.

Watering: Allow soil to dry between waterings.

Fertilize: Monthly when actively growing, every 2 to 3 months otherwise.

Soil: Any general houseplant soil which drains well.

Additional Growing Information:
Kalanchoes are propagated by cuttings. To flower again, they must have at least 14 hours of uninterrupted darkness nightly for a period of 3 months. Placing your plant nightly in a closet or in a room not lighted during the night will work well.

PURPLE SCALLOPS
Kalanchoe fedtschenkoi

The bluish leaves have scalloped purple margins. Clusters of nodding, coral flowers are clasped in sheaths of pale lilac.

Foliage Kalanchoes

COCONUT PALMS
Kalanchoe x Houghton's Hybrid
Remarkable plant producing small plants at the leaf tips to propagate itself.

VELVET LEAF
Kalanchoe beharensis
Large, coarse textured leaves are produced on the sturdy, shrub like plant.

Caring For Your Foliage Kalanchoe

Temperature: Average to warm (65-90°F, 19-32°C) all year.

Light: Bright light.

Watering: Allow soil to dry between waterings.

Fertilize: Monthly if growing rapidly, every 2-3 months otherwise.

Soil: Any general houseplant soil that permits good drainage.

Additional Growing Information:
All Kalanchoes can be propagated by cuttings; Coconut Palms can also be propagated by the small plants which develop at the leaf tips.

PANDA PLANT ▶
Kalanchoe tomentosa
Velvety leaves in silver with warm brown edging for beautiful contrast.

66

Living Stones *Lithops species*

In nature, Living Stones grow submerged in soil to their tops, camouflaging themselves as rocks. When raised as houseplants they are left exposed to prevent rotting.

Caring For Your Living Stones

Temperature: Average to warm (65-90°F, 19-32°C) all year.

Light: Bright light.

Watering: Allow soil to dry completely between infrequent, light waterings (about every 3 weeks) during the summer dormant period: approximately June through August. Water more frequently the rest of the year, but allow soil to dry between waterings.

Fertilize: Monthly while growing, none while dormant.

Soil: A very sandy, quick draining mixture of ⅔ coarse sand and ⅓ general houseplant soil.

Additional Growing Information: Living Stones are native to the Southern Hemisphere, and hence their growing season is reversed and will occur during winter in the northern hemisphere. They may, however, switch over to a summer growing season after some time, so watch your plants to determine their growing season. Plants entering dormancy will begin forming a papery outer skin.

Pachyphytum

Pachyphytum kimnachii

Flesh leaved succulent with blunted leaf tips marked attractively with red.

Caring For Your Pachyphytum

Temperature: Average to warm (65-90°F, 19-32°C) in spring and summer; cool (50-55°F, 10-13°C) in winter.

Light: Bright light.

Watering: Let soil approach dryness in spring and summer; keep drier in fall and winter.

Fertilize: Monthly in spring and summer; none in winter.

Soil: A mixture of equal parts coarse sand and general houseplant soil.

Additional Growing Information: Flowers appear in early spring. Propagated by rooting healthy leaves or by cuttings if available.

Peperomia

Peperomia columella

Caring For Your Peperomia

Temperature: Average to warm (65-90°F, 19-32°C) all year.

Light: Bright light.

Watering: Allow soil to approach dryness between waterings in spring and summer; keep drier in fall and winter.

Fertilize: Every 2 months in spring and summer; none in winter.

Soil: A mixture of equal parts coarse sand and general houseplant soil.

Additional Growing Information:
An extremely slow growing plant. May be propagated from cuttings taken when the plant is actively growing.

Split Rock

Pleiospilos bolusii

South African succulent in the Mesemb group (see introduction).

Caring For Your Split Rock

Temperature: Average to warm (65-90°F, 19-32°C) all year.

Light: Bright light.

Watering: Give frequent, light waterings in spring and summer, as often as soil approaches dryness. Water less often in winter.

Fertilize: Monthly during the growing season; none while dormant.

Soil: A mixture of ⅔ coarse sand and ⅓ general houseplant soil.

Additional Growing Information: An adaptable and easily grown succulent which has its growing period during the summer instead of in winter as other Mesembs do.

69

Portulacaria

ELEPHANT BUSH
Portulacaria afra

Upright bushy succulent related to Jade Plant.

Caring For Your Portulacaria

Temperature: Average to warm (65-90°F, 19-32°C) all year.

Light: Bright light is preferred, however Elephant Bush will grow under only moderate light for several months

Watering: Let soil approach dryness between waterings in spring and summer; every 2-3 months in fall and winter.

Soil: A mixture of equal parts coarse sand and general houseplant soil.

Additional Growing Information: Propagated by cuttings taken when actively growing.

RAINBOW BUSH
Portulacaria afra variegata

Interesting variegated form of the green parent.

WHITE SANSEVIERIA
Sansevieria trifasciata 'Bantel's Sensation'

Unique Snake Plant brilliantly striped in silver and green.

Caring For Your Snake Plant

Temperature: Average to warm (65-90°F, 19-32°C) all year is best, but will tolerate a wide range of temperatures.

Light: Snake Plants which are completely green will live in dim light. Variegated types such as White Sansevieria need moderate light.

Watering: Snake Plants should be allowed to dry out between waterings, but will survive both underwatering and over-watering when grown under warm conditions.

Fertilize: Every three months.

Soil: Any general houseplant potting soil.

Additional Growing Information: Sansevierias are among the most indestructible of all houseplants, existing under conditions which would kill many other plants. Propagate by division, breaking off suckers, or rooting a cross section of leaf.

Snake Plants

BIRDSNEST SANSEVIERIA
Sansevieria trifasciata 'Hahnii'

Dwarf type Snake Plant growing to a height of about 6" (15 cm).

71

PYGMY JOSHUA TREE Upper far left
Sedum multiceps

An unusual tree type Sedum

VARIEGATED
CARPET SEDUM Upper left
Sedum lineare variegatum

Pale green leaves frosted and edged white highlight any room.

Caring For Your Sedum

Temperature: Average to warm (65°F, 19°C and up) all year. A cooler period in winter of 55-60°F (13-18°C) is beneficial.

Light: Bright light.

Watering: Let soil approach dryness between waterings in spring and summer; keep drier in fall and winter.

Fertilize: Monthly in spring and summer. Every three months in fall and winter.

Soil: Any general houseplant potting soil.

Additional Growing Information:
All Sedums may be propagated from cuttings, whether they are upright or vining types. Christmas Cheers and Burro's Tail will also make new plants from rooted leaves.

BURRO'S TAIL Upper right
Sedum morganianum

Pendulous stems are clad in grey-green teardrop leaves.

CHRISTMAS CHEERS Lower right
Sedum rubrotinctum

Popular succulent whose blunted green leaves turn coppery red in strong sunlight.

CARPET SEDUM Lower far left
Sedum sarmentosum

Cascading succulent for indoor or summertime outdoor use.

OLD MAN'S BONES Lower left
Sedum divergens

Knob-shaped leaves thickly set on creeping stems.

Sempervivum 'Purple Beauty'

Another brightly colored Hen and Chicks for windowsill or patio.

Sempervivum x pilosella

Fresh green rosettes tipped maroon.

Sempervivum x Sanford hybrid

A lovely combination of rose and maroon leaves makes this Hen and Chicks almost flowerlike.

Hen & Chicks

Caring For Your Hen and Chicks

Temperature: Tolerant, from 100°F (38°C) in summer to far below freezing in winter.

Light: Bright light.

Watering: Allow soil to approach dryness between waterings in spring and summer; keep drier in winter indoors or do not water at all if kept in below freezing temperatures outdoors.

Fertilize: Monthly from spring through summer as soon as new growth begins; none in winter.

Soil: Garden soil or general houseplant potting soil.

Additional Growing Information:
Hen and Chicks are propagated by rooting the numerous sucker plants (chicks) appearing at the base of larger plants.

Although they are hardy in most northern climates, Hen and Chicks should be gradually adjusted to cold temperatures by being grown outdoors from at least late summer.

COBWEB HOUSELEEK ▼
Sempervivum arachnoideum

The leaf tips and new growth of Cobweb Houseleek are covered with white filaments resembling spiderwebs.

VARIEGATED WAX IVY
Senecio macroglossus variegatus

Hanging basket favorite with leathery green and white leaves.

STRING OF PEAS
Senecio rowleyanus

Unique succulent with bead-like leaves along the trailing stems.

Senecio

Caring For Your Senecio

Temperature: Average to warm (65-90°F, 19-32°C) all year.

Light: String of Peas and Vertical Leaf need bright light. Variegated Wax Ivy will grow with only moderate light.

Watering: Allow soil to approach dryness between waterings.

Fertilize: Monthly in spring and summer; every 3 months in fall and winter.

Soil: Any general houseplant potting soil.

Additional Growing Information: Senecios are propagated by cuttings taken while the plants are actively growing.

◄ VERTICAL LEAF
Senecio crassissimus

Novelty plant for indoor decoration, its curious leaves situated vertically along the stems.

HAIRY STARFISH FLOWER
Stapelia nobilis

Magnificent flowering plant, the large (14", 35 cm) flowers lightly lined with crimson and fringed with silky hairs.

Caring For Your Starfish Flower

Temperature: Average to warm (65-90°F, 19-32°C) all year.

Light: Bright light.

Watering: Allow soil to approach dryness between waterings in spring and summer; keep drier in fall and winter.

Fertilize: Monthly from spring through summer; none in winter.

Soil: A mixture of equal parts coarse sand and general houseplant soil.

Additional Growing Information: Starfish Flowers are propagated from cuttings taken in summer or from seed.

Starfish Flowers

CARRION FLOWER
Stapelia variegata

Aptly named, since the flowers, though quite beautiful, have the odor of rotting meat.

Index

Acknowledgements 2
Adjusting Succulents to Indoor Conditions 4
Adromischus cooperi 42
Adromischus rupicolus 42
Aeonium arboreum var. atropurpureum 43
Aeonium canariense 43
Aeonium decorum 43
African Milk Tree *(Euphorbia trigona)* 57
Agave angustifolia cv. marginata 44
Agave Cactus *(Leuchtenbergia principis)* 26
Agave univittata 45
Agave victoriae-reginae 45
Aloe arborescens 47
Aloe barbadensis (vera) 47
Aloe mitriformis 46
Aloe variegata 46
Aphids 12
Apple Cacti *(Cereus)* 18
Ariocarpus fissuratus 15
Artichoke Cactus *(Obregonia denegrii)* 34
Artificial Light 5
Astrophytum asterias 16
Astrophytum capricorne v. minor 17
Astrophytum myriostigma 17
Astrophytum ornatum 16
Baby Toes *(Fenestraria rhopalophylla)* 58
Ball Cacti *(Notocactus)* 32-33
Barbados Gooseberry *(Pereskia aculeata)* 37
Beaucarnea recurvata 48
Birdsnest Cactus *(Mammillaria camptotricha)* 29
Birdsnest Sansevieria *(Sansevieria trifasciata 'Hahnii')* 71
Bishop's Cap *(Astrophytum myriostigma)* 17
Black-spined Prickly Pear *(Opuntia violacea v. macrocentra)* 35
Black Tree Aeonium *(Aeonium arboreum var. atropurpureum)* 43
Botanical Naming 2-3
Bowiea volubilis 49
Brain Cactus *(Echinofossulocactus species)* 22
Bruch's Chin Cactus *(Gymnocalycium bruchii)* 25
Bunny Ears *(Opuntia microdasys)* 35
Burro's Tail *(Sedum morganianum)* 73
Buying Cacti and Succulents 3
Calico Hearts *(Adromischus rupicolus)* 42
Candelabra Aloe *(Aloe arborescens)* 47
Candelabra Euphorbia *(Euphorbia lactea)* 56
Carnegiea gigantea 17
Carpet Sedum *(Sedum sarmentosum)* 72
Carrion Flower *(Stapelia variegata)* 77
Cereus peruvianus 18
Cereus peruvianus-monstrose dwarf 18
Chamaecereus silvestri 19
Chin Cacti *(Gymnocalycium)* 25
Christmas Cactus *(Zygocactus truncatus)* 40-41

Christmas Cheer *(Zygocactus truncatus 'Christmas Cheer')* 40
Christmas Cheers *(Sedum rubrotinctum)*
Cinnamon Cactus *(Opuntia rufida)* 35
Cleistocactus strausii 19
Climbing Onion *(Bowiea volubilis)* 49
Cobweb Houseleek *(Sempervivum arachnoideum)* 75
Cockleburs *(Huernia hybrid)* 63
Coconut Palms *(Kalanchoe x Houghton Hybrid)* 66
Column Cactus *(Cereus peruvianus)* 18
Column Peperomia *(Peperomia columella)* 69
Cone Plant *(Conophytum meyeri)* 49
Conophytum meyeri 49
Containers 8
Copper Pinwheel *(Aeonium decorum)* 4?
Coral Bells *(Cotyledon orbiculata)* 50
Coryphantha elephantidens 20
Cotyledon macrantha 50
Cotyledon orbiculata 50
Crassula falcata 52
Crassula lycopodioides 53
Crassula perforata 53
Crassula portulacea (argentea) 51
Crassula portulacea minima 51
Crassula portulacea 'Tricolor Jade' 51
Cream Lace Cactus *(Echinocereus reiche bachii v. fitchii)* 21
Crown Cacti *(Rebutia)* 38
Crown of Thorns *(Euphorbia milii v. splendens)* 55
Crested Cow's Horn *(Euphorbia grandico cv. cristata)* 56
Cresting 12
Curiosity Plant *(Cereus peruvianus-monstrose dwarf)* 18
Definition of Cacti and Succulents 2
Devil's Head *(Homalocephala texensis)*
Dwarf Chin Cacti *(Gymnocalycium)* 25
Dwarf Turk's Cap *(Melocactus matazanus*
Easter Cactus *(Rhipsalidopsis)* 39
Echeveria dactylifera 54
Echeveria hybrid 54
Echeveria pubescens 54
Echinocactus grusonii 20
Echinocereus engelmannii 21
Echinocereus pectinatus v. neomexicanus 21
Echinocereus reichenbachii v. fitchii 21
Echinofossulocactus species 22
Echinopsis 'Haku Jo' 22
Elephant Bush *(Portulacaria afra)* 70
Elephant's Tooth *(Coryphantha elephantidens)* 20
Epiphyllum hybrid 23
Epiphyllum 'Paul de Longpre' 23
Epiphyllum 'Showboat' 23
Espostoa lanata 24

horbia cereiformis 57
horbia grandicornis cv. cristata 56
horbia hybrid (lophogona x milii v.
)lendens) 55
horbia lactea 56
horbia milii v. splendens 55
horbia pugniformis 57
horbia tirucalli 57
horbia trigona 57
's Pin Cactus (Opuntia subulata) 35
y Washboard (Haworthia limifolia) 60
caria hybrid 58
ther Cactus (Mammillaria plumosa) 30
estraria rhopalophylla 58
ocactus acanthodes 24
ilizer 24
ball Kalanchoe (Kalanchoe 'Fuerball') 64
Barrel (Ferocactus acanthodes) 24
wering of Cacti 11
teria hybrid 59
st Plant (Graptopetalum
araguayense) 59
nt Crown of Thorns (Euphorbia hybrid) 55
nt Saguaro (Carnegiea gigantea) 17
nt Velvet Rose (Aeonium canariense) 43
t's Horn (Astrophytum capricorne v.
inor) 17
den Ball (Notocactus leninghausii) 33
den Barrel (Echinocactus grusonii) 20
den Stars (Mammillaria elongata) 30
dtooth Aloe (Aloe mitriformis) 46
fted Cacti 41
ptopetalum paraguayense 59
enovia dodrentalis (gracilis) 60
wth Cycles in Cacti and Succulents 4-5
nnocalycium baldianum 25
nnocalycium bruchii 25
nnocalycium mihanovichii friedrichii 25
nnocalycium quehlianum 25
ry Starfish Flower (Stapelia nobilis) 77
ku Jo (Echinopsis 'Haku Jo') 22
worthia hybrid 61
worthia limifolia 61
worthia mucronata 61
worthia subfasciata 60
lgehog Cacti (Echinocereus) 21
n and Chicks (Sempervivum) 74-75
malocephala texensis 26
ya carnosa compacta 'Mauna Loa' 62
ya carnosa rubra 62
ernia hybrid (pillansii x macrocarpa) 63
ects 78
oduction 2
h Rose (Greenovia dodrentalis) 60
le Plant (Crassula portulacea) 51
anchoe beharensis 66
anchoe fedtschenkoi 65
anchoe 'Fuerball' 64
anchoe x 'Houghton's Hybrid' 66
anchoe manginii 65
anchoe tomentosa 66
nnach's Pachyphytum (Pachyphytum
imnachii) 68

Kris Kringle (Zygocactus truncatus
   'Kris Kringle' 40
Leuchtenbergia principis 26
Light 5
Lithops species 67
Little Zebra Plant (Haworthia subfasciata) 60
Living Rock (Ariocarpus fissuratus) 15
Living Stones (Lithops species) 67
Lophocereus schottii monstrosus 27
Low Light 78
Lura Lei® (Hoya carnosa compacta
   'Mauna Loa' 62
Mammillaria bocasana 28
Mammillaria camptotricha 29
Mammillaria candida v. caespitosa 29
Mammillaria elongata 30
Mammillaria hahniana 28
Mammillaria parkinsonii 28
Mammillaria plumosa 30
Mammillaria polyedra 29
Mammillaria rhodantha 30
Mealy Bugs 12
Medicinal Aloe (Aloe barbadensis) 47
Medusa's Head (Euphorbia pugniformis) 57
Melocactus matazanus 31
Melocactus obtusipetalus 31
Miniature Jade Plant (Crassula portulacea
   minima) 51
Monstrose Totem Pole (Lophocereus
   schottii monstrosus) 27
Necklace Vine (Crassula perforata) 53
Nematodes 12
Neoporteria gerocephala 32
Notocactus apricus 32
Notocactus haselbergii 33
Notocactus leninghausii 33
Notocactus scopa 33
Obregonia denegrii 34
Old Lady Cactus (Mammillaria hahniana) 28
Old Man of the Andes (Oreocereus
   celsianus 36
Old Mans Bones (Sedum divergens) 72
Opuntia microdasys 35
Opuntia paediophylla 34
Opuntia rufida 35
Opuntia subulata 35
Opuntia violacea v. macrocentra 35
Orchid Cacti (see Epiphyllum)
Oreocereus celsianus 36
Oreocereus trollii 36
Outdoor Care 9
Owl's Eyes (Mammillaria parkinsonii) 28
Ox Tongue (Gasteria hybrid) 59
Pachyphytum kimnachii 68
Panda Plant (Kalanchoe tomentosa) 66
Paper Spine (Opuntia paediophylla) 34
Partridge Breast Aloe (Aloe variegata) 46
Peanut Cactus (Chamaecereus silverstri) 19
Pencil Euphorbia (Euphorbia tirucalli) 57
Peperomia columella 69
Pereskia aculeata 37
Peruvian Old Man (Espostoa lanata) 24
Pilosocereus maxonii 37

Index Continued

Pincushion Cacti *(Mammillaria)* 28-30
Pleiospilos bolusii 69
Plover Eggs *(Adromischus cooperi)* 42
Pony Tail Palm *(Beaucarnea recurvata)* 48
Portulacaria afra 70
Portulacaria afra variegata 70
Powder Puff *(Mammillaria bocasana)* 28
Propagation 9-10
Propeller Plant *(Crassula falcata)* 52
Princess Pine *(Crassula lycopodioides)* 53
Purple Scallops *(Kalanchoe fedtschenkoi)* 65
Pygmy Joshua Tree *(Sedum multiceps)* 72
Queen Agave *(Agave victoriae-reginae)* 45
Rainbow Bush *(Portulacaria afra variegata)* 70
Rainbow Cactus *(Echinocereus pectinatus v. neomexicanus)* 21
Rainbow Pincushion *(Mammillaria rhodantha)* 30
Rebutia heliosa 38
Rebutia krainziana 38
Rebutia senilis hybrid 38
Repotting 8
Rhipsalidopsis cv. 'Andrae 39
Rhipsalidopsis rosea 39
Root Mealy Bugs 12
Rose Easter Cactus *(Rhipsalidopsis rosea)* 39
Rose Plaid Cactus *(Gymnocalycium mihanovichii friedrichii* 25
Rot 12
Saguaro *(Carnegiea gigantea)* 17
Sand Dollar *(Astrophytum asterias)* 16
Sansevieria trifasciata 'Bantel's Sensation' 71
Sansevieria trifasciata 'Hahnii' 71
Scale 12
Scarlet Ball *(Notocactus haselbergii)* 33
Scarlet Bells *(Cotyledon macrantha)* 50
Scarlet Easter Cactus *(Rhipsalidopsis cv. 'Andrae'* 39
Schlumbergera (see *Zygocactus)*
Sedum divergens 72
Sedum lineare variegaum 72
Sedum morganianum 73
Sedum multiceps 72
Sedum rubrotinctum 73
Sedum sarmentosum 72
Sempervivum arachnoideum 75
Sempervivum x pilosella 74
Sempervivum x 'Purple Beauty' 75

Sempervivum x Sandford hybrid 75
Senecio crassissimus 76
Senecio macroglossus variegatus 76
Senecio rowleyanus 76
Silver Ball *(Notocactus scopa)* 33
Silver Torch *(Cleistocactus strausii)* 19
Snake Plants *(Sansevieria)*
Snowball Pincushion *(Mammillaria canc v. caespitosa)* 29
Soils 8
Spider Mites 12
Split Rock *(Pleiospilos bolusii)* 69
Stapelia nobilis 77
Stapelia variegata 77
Star Cactus *(Astrophytum)* 16-17
Star Cactus *(Astrophytum ornatum)* 16
Starfish Flower *(Stapelia)* 77
String of Peas *(Senecio rowleyanus)* 76
Strawberry Hedgehog *(Echinocereus engelmannii)* 21
Sunburn 12
Sun Cap *(Notocactus apricus)* 32
Sun Rebutia *(Rebutia heliosa)* 38
Table of Contents 1
Temperature 7
Tiger Jaws *(Faucaria hybrid)* 58
Turk's Cap *(Melocactus)* 31
Variegated Caribbean Agave *(Agave angustifolia cv. marginata)* 44
Variegated Carpet Sedum *(Sedum linea variegatum)* 72
Variegated Jade Plant *(Crassula portula 'Tricolor Jade')* 51
Variegated Wax Ivy *(Senecio macroglos variegatus)* 76
Variegated Wax Plant *(Hoya carnosa variegata)* 62
Velvet Leaf *(Kalanchoe beharensis)* 66
Vertical Leaf *(Senecio crassissimus)* 76
Water 6
Watering Methods 6
Wax Plants *(Hoya)* 62
Woolly Torch *(Pilosocereus maxonii)* 37
White Christmas *(Zygocactus truncactu 'Alba')* 41
White Sansevieria *(Sansevieria trifascia 'Bantel's Sensation')* 71
Zygocactus truncatus 'Alba' 41
Zygocactus truncatus 'Christmas Cheer'
Zygocactus truncatus 'Kris Kringle' 40